EIGHTH PENTAD UNIVERSAL INTERPRETATION

THE QUEEN DOMINATES THE FEELINGS KEEPER

JOHN J. A. MARTZHALL

Stellar Goddess... Girls from the stars... Queen empresses... are the 9 half-steps constituting 3 tritones, between 2 notes belonging to a tetrachord, a method that manifests "The feelings keeper" inside each person, through the sense of hearing.

Contents

Preface

The nine half-steps constituting three tritones between two melodic notes of a tetrachord in light state, traveled through the BMB DC universe, these nine half-steps together make up the Goddess who acquired the form of nine girls from the stars, who upon arrival to the metaverse of the small blue world they were proclaimed with titles of queen empresses, granted for dominating the feelings inside them, while their knowledge instructs people who enter the metaverse of the small blue world identifying "The feelings keeper" inside each one; Source of poetry "Eighth Pentad Universal interpretation".

Prologue

Soft dactyls were configured with the passing of time, forming warm diligent hands, property of the beauty that came from the sky using the minor scale, nine sublime reasons to observe the stellar reality composition of a Goddess, nine girls from the stars with unique fingerprint; their hands hold imposing tridentis property of the immensity that rides on the waters to the depths of the heart with tritone distance backing the majesty of the nine precious empresses queen as they breathe silencing the ideas of the mind to selectively reflect from their heart the moods imparting their new reality.

1. Attractive eyes - black moon pansy flower

Attractive eyes, gently contemplate in their minds the symmetry of an Ionian tetrachord blooming like a pansy flower whose guardian petals are pigmented scarlet to descend at high speed to the heart of nine empress queens, while reflecting that mood and instinct to Through their human form, Pretty architecture of splendid universal essence like beautiful girls of the stars, their benevolent will allows the feelings keeper to manifest as "Highlight" inside themself.

Black moon pansy flower, the prismatic pentad absorbs light pigmenting yellow petals, "the feelings keeper" constantly reflecting the glorious key signature characteristic of a Phrygian kingdom in nine resplendent golden hearts of a unimaginable electromagnetic power, beautiful belonging of each Empress queen whose self control transcends the speed of sound, her cunning attracts attention of twenty-four galaxies in the known universe; pansy flower that in the minds of nine girls from the stars feeds with photovoltaic imagination the absolute mood by their decision to impart a new reality in any unexpected reality-shaking circumstances.

John J A Martzhall

69

2. In the sharp heights – Fascinating Goddess

In the sharp heights a splendid star formation cloud stores twelve key signatures, these are the endowment a fascinating electromagnetic power very close to flat depths whose space is appropriate for twelve other key of twenty-four endowments forged for the stellar Goddess, all are unexpected circumstances of the life, such conducive circumstances, as the nursery of "the feelings keeper". Nine girls from the stars, have the ability to modulate the depths that open in the heights with their universal will, their dominance benevolently pigments "black moon" petals, reflecting the color white in the quickly descending reaction to the heart in the nine empress queens.

Fascinating Goddess of evening sunrises, the beauty of your oriental brightness simultaneously precedes the unconditional rising sun extending over the unison, vital essence of a tender spontaneous smile on the soft lips of nine girls from the stars whose benevolent dominion pigments "the feelings keeper" of gold yellow, the inner beauty in nine glorious Empress queens cunningly persuade that reaction, covering it with an honorable reflection, signature key characteristic of the Phrygian kingdom whose color frequency transforms moods and instincts, by decision of the Queen empress to selectively absorb that idea of reality in changing circumstances of real life.

John J A Martzhall
69

3. Incandescent ionian stellar strength – Light in the twelfth meridion

Incandescent ionian stellar strength that sustains the better elements from the seven kingdoms, incorporated by universal will to the nine girls from the stars, for dominate in the wide field of the mind, the overflowing imagination craved by the reaction, keeping that feel in unexpected circumstances. Iris of fire supernatural, warm light white dispersed by the prismatic "black moon" feeding the feelings keeper with colorful ideas; nine fascinating blossoming minds of guardian petals whose pigment are moods and instincts occupying the beautiful heart of the nine empress queens by her decision to selectively absorb any idea of reality, while they cunningly dominate the the feelings keeper using the silence of thoughts.

Light in the twelfth meridion, day and night, bearer of chromatic reactions with innumerable combinations, being pansies flowered in the wide field that constitutes the beautiful mind belonging to each empress queen, the cunning with the silence of the thoughts persuade "the feelings keeper", identifying the reflected domain by the nine girls from the stars, who constantly pigment the guardian petals willingly imparting a new reality with their selective moods.

John J A Martzhall
69

4. Synchronism of time - Heights and depths

Synchronism of time brings back the golden weave canvas that gently extends from the heights, a path carved by delicate step of passionate beauty, cradle of Goddess born in nine girls from the stars, they contemplate in their hearts "the feelings keeper" day and night, like petals of the pansy flower, that by their will have been dominated cunningly by the silence of thoughts, while their breathe; Over time each Empress queen understood to live with herself, in a world whose heart pigmented with "black moon" petals ignores the existence of "the feelings keeper" inside itself. Heights and depths modulated by fascinating polaris brightness interpreted by the beautiful gaze of nine precious girls of the stars as they dominate within themselves a docile feelings keeper; Nine empress queens contemplate the art of an unconditional doric kingdom that pigments orange the black moon pentachord; A new reality, is to understand that you cunningly perceive "the feelings keeper" as a blooming of spring in the light of your senses, through people, places or objects that inevitably infuse thoughts in your mind transformed into moods and instincts in your heart; Cunning with the silence of thoughts will persuade "the feelings keeper".

John J. A. Martzhall

69

5. Singular warmth - blooming new moon

Singular warmth from the expected winter rain, one thousand six hundred and eighty gleams came from the red-hot forge while the 24 key signatures were adequate to cover a Goddess; many shining with experience locria others with aeolian wisdom, without hesitation some more with sincerity Mixolidia, loving Lydians, glorious Phrygians, passionate Dorians and strong Ionians ... they touched the earth diligently, terracotta men and women, of steel inside and with the admirable knowledge of the art made as a pendant, whose only purpose with its anticipated arrival is to assist the nine beautiful girls from the stars, in dissuading humanity to dominate "the feelings keeper" inhabiting each person.

Blooming new moon, black sapphires of great value, privilege of aeolian wisdom characterizing the precious mind in every girl from the stars whose benevolent dominion of the feelings keeper while they breathe fascinatingly harmonizes pansies and feelings in the docile black moon by reflect blue petals in nine beautiful golden hearts.

John J A Martzhall

69

6. Essential cunning – Dome of predisposed polyphonies

Essential cunning, source of skill, formulate of the nine empress queens to understand they are not that reaction flourished in milliseconds of sixteenth note as a feelings keeper; Splendid benefit, like the morning dew building with ideas the pansies of a new reality, being a resplendent loveliness of the nine girls from the stars, by avoiding reflecting black moon pigmented petals pretending to be absolute in unexpected real life circumstances that can be handled.

Dome of predisposed polyphonies, scarlet pigmented Ionian strength frequency; Self-coexistence discipline instructed by helios at nine precious diamonds unique in the immensity of the universe for their essential beauty and passionately incorporated in each beautiful form adopted by the Goddess, being nine girls from the stars whose unequaled electromagnetic power transform any solar storm caused by a uncontrolled black moon, flowered in different unexpected circumstances of life; cunning with the silence of thoughts will persuade "the feelings keeper".

John J A Martzhall

69

7. Unexpected circumstances - Wind instruments

Unexpected circumstances of real life, fantastic show with an audience in the wide field of the universal mind where Gods take root who descend speed to the heart of the earth ; Beautiful Goddess, while you traveled through two tetrachords, the cian blue sky was decorated with fascinating electromagnetic power when nine stars descended entering the heart of the show adopting a subtle figure in nine treasured girls with the title of empress queens whose own script product of their nature invaluable, is to dominate with benevolence "the feelings keeper" that inhabits inside each empress queen.

Wind instruments that interpret the autumnal polyphony preceding winter, beautiful empress queen, the ionian force and the aeolian wisdom pigment violet "the feelings keeper" in your golden heart, while the black moon is fascinated by you self-control, essence treasured in nine precious girls from the stars whose extraordinary strength and wisdom give them a locrian experience being cunning knowledge to identify any flowered reaction in different unexpected circumstances of life.

John J A Martzhall

69

8. A paradisiacal sunrise - Precious Goddess

A paradisiacal sunrise is confirmed on the winter scale, whose unbridled degrees testify how twenty-four galaxies showed the way to a Goddess who opens her eyes in her human form, nine empress queens whose nature gave them a wonderful superhuman quality; fascinating is the ability of nine girls of the stars to dominate the guardian of feelings, the cunning with the silence of thoughts will persuade "the feelings keeper".

Precious Goddess that is contemplated in each queen empress with beautiful physical silhouettes when the nine girls from the stars dominate "the feelings keeper" within themselves, adapting with balance when shaking reality; Harmoniously molded gold by a magnificent constellation sculptor. Nine girls from the stars have understood the beauty of their human nature being the uncontrolled instinctual magic in the unexplainable beats of her brave heart, caused by any unexpected circumstances of life; Learn to coexist with herself is the right way for empresses queen, the ability to understand different feelings in the heart gave them the benefit of self-control as they breath using the discipline instructed by the experience of the oriental soul who witnessed his birth in the stellar cradle.

John J A Martzhall

69

9. Eyes to the sky - Determinant natural light

Eyes to the sky are opened perceiving a majestic universe that houses such a splendid manifestation contained nine times in precious and priceless girls from the stars, whose incalculable value is compared with the seven harmonies that at their side at all times accompany to the nine empress queens if they need it; their delicate steps extend firmly shaking the reddish and arid surface of the unison, to build their own dream and belong to humanity; nine hearts silence thoughts understanding "they are not their own thoughts or their own feelings"; how modest the perfection of beauty can be in nine beautiful treasures that possess the virtue of a phoenix and yet shed tender and subtle tears transformed into sapphires that shine demonstrating the authenticity of their origin while an unimaginable power is found in the warmth of their hands to reach the goal.

Determinant natural light drawing of fundamental force, precedes seemingly remote flowing melodies, winter rays that draw the eye to the ivory sky, curtain of sincerity mixolidia, attribute of a kingdom, the sensible electromagnetic polyphony from the nine girls of the stars, unveil the rising sun in the heights, complacent dwelling of majestic helium that surrounds with its warm energy, the beautiful natural essence of nine precious diamonds that constitute the art made pendant.

John J A Martzhall
69

10. The violet experience - Docile spring pansy flower

The violet experience, point of departure from a locrian reality molded the consciousness of a Goddess who, as she passed through the galaxies, understood yin and yan as the means to recognize "the feelings keeper" when the beauty of this immensity materializes in unison as nine wonders, whose strength to dominate and persuade transcends by believing in themselves; powerful electromagnetic discharge, reaction of nine wonderful and beautiful girls from the stars that shine in the winter minor scale as they dominate "the feelings keeper".

Docile spring pansy flower that decorates attributes of fine curves outlining beautiful absolute hears in nine empress queens, one of several senses in consciousness, whose purpose perceives the feelings keeper persuaded by the nine girls from the stars when they dominate with benevolence their own reaction, while they impart gleams of a new reality with universal transcendence.

John J A Martzhall

69

11. Ancestral purpose – Day and night nine

Ancestral purpose characteristic of the universal will; the feelings keeper, reaction with uncontrolled purpose in the heart of each person; she docile bows to nine precious stellar bodies that possess the strength granted by the Ionic kingdom; Nine loving girls from the stars whose glorious eyes remain wide open radiating extraordinary electromagnetic power in sincere bright days, their nights are appeased with great experience as they passionately await the next day to wisely dominate to the feelings keeper.

Day and night nine brave hearts of high imperial rank, whose golden glow of infinite magnitude with imperative relevance are discreetly contemplated by the throbbing reaction in the warm chest of the nine Empress queens; artwork made as a pendant with emerald green pigmented petals; the black moon transforms reflecting the inner beauty, valuable attribute of nine girls from the stars when they dominate "the feelings keeper" that blooms in their minds by unexpected circumstances of real life.

John J A Martzhall

69

12. Sunsets that captivate - Sweet silence

Sunsets that captivate with their evening glow, frequency of smiles that flow like the wind from delicate crimson lips belonging to nine beautiful empress queens, revealing their molded golden hearts as they sharpen their perfection for the excellence that day after day is demonstrated in nine girls from the stars through her discipline, characteristic virtue of the united Goddess, used in unexpected circumstances of life to dominate the feelings keeper petals blossoming in the mind as thoughts.

Sweet silence reflected in white bloomed petals, pigmenting the reaction in the symmetry of a pentad "black moon", when nine beautiful empress queens take a deep breath, using cunning as formulated to differentiate themselves from "the feelings keeper"; enchanting brilliance coming from the fascinating loveliness contemplated in the stellar body of the nine girls from the stars, reflects possessing the art made pendant, demonstrating to understand with careful logic when to combine the silence of thoughts in "the feelings keeper", achieving harmonic coherence by balancing their new reality.

John J A Martzhall

69

The Feeling Is Valuable

The feeling is valuable when they enthusiastically pigment castles in the sand made of stainless steel, precious as gold for their gently, no tear of sadness has the potential of a wave to demolish their diamond walls, each one is their own guide, so, it's a structured path with the correct answers; "start over" is perhaps a thought that defines "dominate your feelings", the days are not unfulfilling when you understand that the most valuable moment is right now.